CUL-DE-SAC

CUL-DE-SAC

Daniel MacIvor

Talonbooks
Vancouver

Talonbooks
P.O. Box 2076, Vancouver, British Columbia, Canada V6B 3S3
www.talonbooks.com

Typeset in New Baskerville and printed and bound in Canada.

Third Printing: 2011

The publisher gratefully acknowledges the financial support of the
Canada Council for the Arts; the Government of Canada through the
Book Publishing Industry Development Program; and the Province of
British Columbia through the British Columbia Arts Council for our
publishing activities.

Library and Archives Canada Cataloguing in Publication

MacIvor, Daniel, 1962–
    Cul-de-sac / Daniel MacIvor.

A play.
ISBN 0-88922-515-X

    I. Title.

PS8575.I86C84 2005   C812'.54   C2004-906440-1

ISBN 13: 978-0-88922-515-2

Foreword

Cul-de-sac is the fourth one-man show I have created with Daniel MacIvor.

In the past, the work on each show would begin with Daniel proposing a title, a concern, an obsession, a theme. Daniel and I would meet, and he would read to me from his notebook. The notebook contained scattered ideas, impressions, and proposals for the work to be developed. *Cul-de-sac* was an exception. The big black notebook Daniel brought to our first meeting was blank.

Though the notebook was blank, we knew something about what we wanted to do; we wanted to do a show about neighbourhood, about how people live together, about a specific neighbourhood in which something burns or someone dies, a show about what connects and separates people. Lonely people trying to connect. We wanted to create a little cul-de-sac in a theatre each and every night. The stage was the end of the dead end. Daniel also knew that he wanted to play a number of characters, and it all had something to do with the idea of "transformation."

Our work was to proceed as follows: an initial exploratory workshop in the Backspace at Theatre Passe Muraille, and several months later, a four week workshop in Montreal, where we would present "a work in progress" to a small audience.

Our first rehearsals in Toronto consisted of long, meandering conversations in the theatre, with one of us often complaining about our life while the other played the sage and offered cheap advice. We would then go for coffee (I can't remember who was or wasn't smoking at the time—we weren't drinking). We would come back to the theatre, and Daniel would—on a good day—start to improvise. As he played, he found the voices for a group of nasty teenagers who had formed a rock band named "G-d's cunt" (or "God's C-nt," can't remember which). He spent an afternoon introducing the band with various voices, and we excitedly chattered about the world inhabited by these teenagers; who knew who, who wore what, who lived where (we often find ourselves gossiping about people who don't exist).

One afternoon Daniel did something very funny with a box of tissues.

We spent a few days messing around, playing around, and talking around. We talked a lot about where we were in our lives (often on the edge of despair), with the speaker often pacing about the little stage in the backspace, the listener waiting for his turn to talk. In these early rehearsals we often tell each other secrets (one such secret that I'm not allowed to tell is a part of this story). We talk of fears, hopes, disappointments, desires, the usual. We talk about other projects we are working on.

At that time, Daniel was working on a script for his first feature film, *Past Perfect*. On the evening of the third day of rehearsal, I read the film script. When I came in to the theatre the next day, I told him I thought the script had some problems and asked if he had time before shooting to work on it. He didn't. He was about to shoot a feature film with an under-developed script while *Cul-de-sac* was scheduled for a mere "work in progress" presentation in Montreal in the distant future. As a result, we spent the remainder of our workshop discussing the screenplay. I have no idea if those discussions ended up influencing the movie Daniel eventually made. I do know that they did influence *Cul-de-sac*, by devouring our time and attention.

The Toronto workshop was not fruitful. In fact, I don't think a single invention from those few days of work made it into our final play. Perhaps there was a glimmer of the beginnings of the character Madison.

I have often been asked how to go about making a play. I usually respond, "book a venue." In the case of *Cul-de-sac* our venue had been booked; Usine C in Montreal. Daniel and I understood that we were to be an informal part of the Theatre du Monde Festival. We were to present our "work in progress" in the studio space at Usine C. The show would be attended by a sophisticated audience, small in numbers, that would understand how to suspend judgment for a "work in progress." This was after all the land of Carbone 14 and Robert Lepage. We had four weeks at Usine C to come up with a little something to show people.

In the weeks before our departure we were both very busy with other projects, and had given *Cul-de-sac* little thought.

Upon our arrival in Montreal, we were given an itinerary; a long impressive list of press interviews. We were going to be on the cover of a weekly magazine, and were to be featured in a number of articles. We were, as it turned out, one of three major shows at the Festival du Monde. We were to open *Cul-de-sac* at an international theatre festival in four weeks in a theatre that seats four hundred.

We had no show to show.

We went to work. Our process was quite simple; Daniel sat in a chair, I sat in a chair. I asked him questions. Slowly, or quickly, he would assume a voice, a character, a name, a gender—sometimes I would make a suggestion as to where to place his voice, what to do with his posture, how to amplify a gesture. I would talk to the character (the neighbour) that Daniel was inhabiting. Often, these characters were quite rude.

As Daniel talked, I wrote down what was of interest to me. I would ask simple questions, sometimes leading questions, and Daniel would answer. Often we would end up in a kind of conversation in which the creature Daniel had created would tell intimate stories or flirt with me or insult me or spew out elaborate philosophies or state crude opinions. When we had had enough, I would read Daniel my notes, perhaps editing as I went, perhaps adding, and he would write down what I said in his notebook, again, editing and adding as he went. We would discuss what was funny, what was a possible narrative strategy, what seemed a fruitful motif. We talked about plays we'd done in the past, how this one might differ, what makes theatre interesting, idly talking and talking for hours on end, reflecting, and remembering. The work was productive, although we had no play, nothing remotely like a play. We had Daniel's big black notebook, and I had a big black notebook filled with words.

We began to panic. We decided that we would simply not be ready to present anything, that this international theatre festival was far too visible and reputable an event in which to present a "work in progress." We thought that since we had never done the one-man show *Here Lies Henry* in English in Montreal, we should do it in *Cul-de-sac*'s place. We made a flurry of panicked phone calls to Sherrie Johnson, the producer of the show, to Andy Moro, who had last operated lights for *Here Lies Henry*, to the people in the office at da da kamera to see if they had all the material we would need for *Here Lies Henry*, and to Marie Helene Falcon, the producer of the festival. We spoke to Marie Helene. We proposed that we do *Here Lies Henry*. She was entirely uninterested in our proposition, and insisted that we continue work on *Cul-de-sac*. She reminded us that her audience knew what "work in progress" meant, and that she was very much looking forward to seeing the beginnings of our new play.

Her expression of faith was bone shatteringly disappointing. We had no play, but we had an audience.

Sherrie did most of the negotiating with Marie Helene, although everyone talked to everyone, and we eventually agreed that we would do the show in the main auditorium at Usine C, but would change the seating around so that there would be between 120 and 140 seats. We went back to work. We asked our hosts at Usine C to hang some lights so that we could begin to experiment with design. We played CDs, seeking music for the show. Daniel continued to talk in his chair, I continued to ask questions, and the notebooks continued to fill with possibilities.

The weekend was approaching. I was to go to Toronto to spend time with my children while Daniel was to attempt to write a draft based on the work he had been collecting in his notebook. On Thursday I had dinner with Daniel. We had a beer. Some friends joined us. We had another beer. Daniel bought a pack of cigarettes. He declared that he was going to stay and drink. When Daniel stays to drink, he does so with abandon. I went back to the hotel.

At ten the next morning I was riding my bike along Rue Ontario on my way to the theatre when I saw a strange looking gentleman on a bicycle, his eyes wide, pupils dilated, face pale. It was Daniel. He stopped in front of me. He explained that he had been in an after hours bar after hours and had left his orange bag unattended, and in those few moments it was stolen. His black notebook was in the bag. He had been riding back and forth along Rue Ontario looking for his notebook, rummaging in trash cans throughout the neighbourhood with the hope that the thief had no use for notebooks and had tossed it in the garbage, or had taken whatever valuables (including Daniel's watch) and thrown the orange bag away. The notebook was not to be found. Daniel had fallen off the wagon and he was feeling guilty, ashamed, and hung over.

It was little over two weeks before our work in progress was to be presented, and we did not have the document that would form the basis of the performance. Over the next two days, we attempted to reconstruct his notes from my notes; a desperately laborious effort and a desperately uninspired one. We were soaked in worry.

At the end of the two days Daniel had reconstructed his notes, and we had the beginnings of characters, some good lines, some thoughts on what would happen in this *Cul-de-sac*, who lived there, what the people might say. We had an opera buff, an autistic boy, the boy's sister, and their father the lawyer. We had a couple from Cape Breton who talked constantly about sex and barbecues, we had an old guy who was dangerously similar to an old guy we had in our last play. We were also interested in an article Daniel found in a local paper that told the story of two neighbours who were battling over a property line. Also with us in Montreal at that time was Amiel Goldstein, a young man we both very much respected. He was there as an apprentice/assistant. He was asked to do a little research on Asperger's, HIV, lawyer lingo, etc … And I had to go to Toronto.

And so, in the next several days, as I returned to the bosom of my family, Daniel lived his own drama as he furiously wrote a play. *Cul-de-sac* was born. More importantly, Daniel's night on the town spawned a new character, Eric. He was born the night Daniel stayed out too late, born of Daniel's shame, frustration, fear, and anger at the bastard who stole his bag and all the stuff in it—like the black notebook and his watch.

Daniel had also fallen upon the central event of the play.

In the meantime, we continued giving interviews. The main theme of those interviews was "process," and we stressed over and over again that we were doing a "work in progress."

We moved into the theatre. We had a script to work from—all of the characters in the finished version of *Cul-de-sac* already existed—and we had an extremely clever idea: Leonard, the central character, would never appear. He was only talked about. We learned about him solely through what the neighbours had to say.

Rehearsal continued. One night, about three days before our opening, we had an idea as to how we would present the play; Daniel would sit at a long table and the play would be like a series of interviews, a kind of documentary, with each of the characters in turn accounting for the events of that murderous night. We brought a long table on stage, Daniel sat behind it and read through the text. Not so interesting. We tried it a number of different ways, but each time he read the text it felt utterly inconsequential. We were weak with despair.

Sherrie Johnson had arrived in Montreal, and was aware of the difficulties we were having. There was not much she could do. Daniel was going to be on a stage in front of 140 people very soon.

I walked home with him that evening. We tried desperately to figure out what it was the play needed. For forty minutes he made me laugh, throwing out one wild proposition after another, one idea after another, improvising on one verbal hook after another, falling into one vivid voice after another, each voice insane, each shatteringly panicked and funny, but not one word useful to us.

That night in our hotel I had a discussion with Sherrie on the telephone. I told her that we did not have a show, and I didn't think we would have one in two days. She calmly said, "If you want to cancel the opening, that's fine, as long as you take responsibility for it." She said the right thing. She provoked me. I was determined to find a solution. I quickly concluded that Leonard needed a voice. The conceit of the central character never speaking was not working. He needed to speak, and he needed to be the centre of the show. I spent the night going over it, making sure that such a shift in the form of the play would work, that it made sense, that it was elegant enough as an idea that Daniel could act upon it in a short time. Daniel was in rough shape. I had to be searingly clear with him.

At seven the next morning I went to his room. I told him what I thought. He was begrudgingly receptive. We talked about what kind of rewrites he might do. He agreed to try. I went back to my room, and for the next fifteen minutes I heard noises— things hitting the wall, cries of despair. Daniel was having a tantrum in the room next door. Then the noises subsided, and I went to sleep.

While I slept, and over the next ten hours, the voice of Leonard, the five-minute "nooooo," and the time structure of *Cul-de-sac* were invented by a feverish and all too awake Daniel MacIvor.

The next day the work continued; Daniel wrote, Amiel researched Gilbert and Sullivan, lights were hung, Daniel wrote and memorized, wrote and memorized, a stage was built, Kim Purtell and I cued the lights as Richard Feren built the sound, the panic peeked, and then, suddenly, 140 people came to Usine C, and sat down, all looking in the same direction, into our *Cul-de-sac.* Daniel had somehow learned the text. He performed it with incredible command. The show ended, and people applauded. Then they stood, and continued applauding.

In the ensuing year we performed *Cul-de-sac* in Philadelphia, Antigonish, and Toronto. In each city we worked on the play. We reassessed text, performance, lights, and sound. We refined verbal rhythms, clarified character and tone, developed details in Leonard's world. Daniel found increasing confidence with his performance, and on the surface the play was driven less and less by fear. Nonetheless, the essence of the play that exploded into life in Montreal changed very little. Daniel gave birth to *Cul-de-sac* in a heightened state of fear, a fear that is not unusual for any person who presents their work to the public, to a very large neighbourhood. It is a fear that is familiar to most people, it is a fear of the question, "What will the neighbours say?" From the point of view of the play's central character Leonard, *Cul-de-sac* is an answer to that question.

—Daniel Brooks

Cul-de-sac was first performed in May 2002 at Usine C in Montreal, Quebec as part of Theatre du Monde with the following cast and crew:

Text and Performance: Daniel MacIvor
Director and Dramaturgy: Daniel Brooks
Lighting Design: Kim Purtell
Sound and Music: Richard Feren
Assistant Director: Amiel Gladstone

Song: "If You See My Love," written by Mary Margaret O'Hara, used by permission of the artist.

*A storm builds. Lightning flashes. Rain
subsides. Light up.*

LEONARD:

Interesting.

I've always been a sucker for an interesting
story.

I mean I don't know if it's going to be
interesting to you, I don't know you. It's
interesting to me because it happened to me.
I mean it wasn't even all that interesting to
me really. It was one of those things you
approach thinking, "oh this is going to be
interesting," and then when it's happening
you think "this is not interesting at all," and
then you just go through with it in hopes that
it will be interesting in the telling. But there's
not really that much to tell. Oh great, there's
not much to tell and not how long in ...

He checks his watch.

Oh I shouldn't have that on.

He takes off the watch.

That's evidence. It used to be mine. Now
it's evidence.

He pockets the watch.

(he sings the theme song to "Law and Order")
Do-do-do-do-do. "Law and Order." I can
understand if you didn't get that. Apparently
I'm somewhat tone deaf. If someone can be
"somewhat" tone deaf.

Note: whenever LEONARD says a word which
is written in quotations he makes a
"quotations" gesture with his fingers.
Pause.

My first mistake was leaving the house.

Well no, my first mistake *that night* was
leaving the house, if we're going to talk about
first mistakes we're going to have to go back a
lot farther than that. In which case my first
mistake would probably be not trying harder
to like hockey.

I don't like hockey. Can you tell? Well I
should hope so, what do you think this is? An
accent? What am I, Australian? I always
thought of Australians being gay because they
were so obsessed with Barbies and so was I!

No I don't like hockey.

I like the costumes. But those shoes?

Pause.

Or maybe my first mistake was trying to
pretend I didn't need anybody. But I do.

Or maybe my first mistake was not realizing
that sophistication was something you could

develop, as opposed to, you know, be "born with." I never did get that.

You all seem pretty sophisticated. I mean I don't know you but, just you know, the "vibe." Well clearly you're sophisticated, you're the type of people who attend a "cultural event." I was never much for cultural events. I was more movies. Not even really … I was more HGTV. Oh, but one time I saw Lena Horne. That was you know … Oh and I saw Bonnie Raitt. But that was more—

Takes lighter from pocket and holds it aloft and lit—then pockets lighter.

Oh and I saw … what was her name? She had a big hit in the '80s.

The concert was packed. You know, that song: (*sings*) "We … " No. (*sings*) "You … " Whatever. And twenty-five bucks to get in. And back then. Oh well what's twenty-five bucks today. Nothing to die over.

Note: the price "twenty-five bucks" recurs through the piece. This number should be the highest ticket price the audience has paid to see Cul-de-sac.

No, in terms of "cultural events" my "entertainment dollar" was more spent at a little place called The Drive Shaft. It was an "alternative space," which was a phrase they developed in the '90s to replace "seedy dive." But it was "home."

(*To himself: remaking quotation gesture with his fingers*) Stop that.

I do that too much. It kind of takes over. Gets into "everything." A simple greeting becomes Hi "how are you?" Oh "Fine." Stop it! It's on my list. Was.

No but The Drive Shaft could be interesting. Especially on Sunday nights they used to have these variety shows with local … (*He can't help himself, he makes the gesture*) "talent."

You know, drag queens, S and M fashion shows, the occasional dancer.

Which brings me to my story. Which is a little on the embarrassing side. But what the heck. It is my story. Of course there are people who say there's only one story and everything else is a variation. You know variations like: a man against the world, a young girl comes of age, a lonely soul loses his cat, two neighbours fight about a property line, a young nobleman is accidentally raised by a band of soft-hearted orphan pirates. Just variations on: the hero and the journey and the hero has to say yes to the journey because there's no journey if the hero says "nooooooo" (*cough*). And those same people also say it's not about the story anyway, it's really about the purpose of the story. And if that were true and you were to ask me, I'd have to say the purpose of the story was something to do with something about the potential for, the desire to, believe in, the possibility of, transformation. Transformation.

You know what is interesting? I lived in this neighbourhood for fifteen years as a person and I had more impact in my last five minutes as a sound.

Thunder—light/sound shift.

2:01 AM. Sunday night. It's raining. It had been a beautiful spring Sunday with summer just coming into view—eager to spread her lazy smile across the well-kept lawns and budding gardens of the neighbourhood. But now it's night and now it's raining. The street is still. The Bickerson house is dark—but behind the open bedroom window he lies calmly sleepless—jousting with memory as he does most nights.

Across the street the Walshes are awake. Joy and Eddy. Eddy is upstairs pretending to be asleep in anticipation of Joy coming up to bed. Joy is downstairs in the den hoping the scary movie will end, desperate to get upstairs to Eddy, but not being able to turn off the movie until she finds out who did it.

The nicest house is bright—Samuel and Virginia. Samuel has risen and gone downstairs in search of the last leftover portion of chocolate pudding. Virginia is upstairs in her office grading papers, wishing she were working on her memoirs, kicking herself for having eaten the last of the last leftover portion of chocolate pudding.

The Saeeds are away for the weekend. Their house is dark but the radio is left on as a tepid security measure against faint-hearted thieves.

The empty house is empty still—but apparently a young couple with children has made an offer and everyone is waiting for the bank.

My house—we'll get to that later.

The Turner house. Ken Turner is asleep on top of the covers, his glasses still on, dossiers for tomorrow's court case spread open across his lap. And in her basement bedroom—her fortress of defiance—his daughter Madison lies still but fully awake. The rain picks up. Madison counts the drops as they plip and plop from the leaky eavestrough onto the empty can of catfood outside her basement bedroom window and thinks about her novel. She's been working on her novel since she was eleven. She's thirteen now. Her novel is called *The Balsawood Astronaut.* Every night it would come to her in her dreams and every morning she would diligently write the chapter in her journal. That all ended after Christmas when her journal was stolen. It didn't really matter anyway since her plan had been to finish the novel and burn the journal. Now she just leaves the chapters in her dreams. The rain slows down. Between the drops Madison chants "The balsawood astronaut … the balsawood astronaut … the balsawood astronaut … " In hopes that the words would become sounds which would envelop her in sleep and into another adventure. And it begins to work: just as the balsawood astronaut is strapped into his seat and the rocket is about to be launched for his first trip into space—his mission to Jupiter— and all systems are go and the engines fire … she hears it.

A long kind of low kind of strange kind of moan kind of sound. It seems to travel along the ground and into her basement bedroom window, along the concrete wall beside her desk where the lamp is off but still warm from where she was studying for her math test, along the wall behind her bed and out the window on the other side of her basement bedroom. The sound changes now—it rakes slightly up and bounces off the empty house, and into the tree in the front yard, moving through the wet branches gaining a kind of slippery momentum, leaping across the street and landing on the Walshes' roof, slithering down the shingles, and seeping … seeping … seeping … seeping … through the siding. It's 2:02 AM.

JOY:

(*to audience*) Excuse me.

Light shift.

Excuse me. Excuse me, I'm sorry to interrupt but it was 1:30. I remember. I remember I remember because I remember hearing the sound and turning over in bed and looking at the clock radio as soon as I heard it. It was 1:30.

EDDY:

It wasn't 1:30 Joy, you weren't even in bed at 1:30.

JOY:

Shut up Eddy I was so.

EDDY:

You were not, you were still downstairs watching the end of that stupid movie you made me rent.

JOY:

I didn't make you rent it.

EDDY:

You did so, you told me to rent something scary, I don't like scary movies.

JOY:

Well neither do I.

EDDY:

Then why did you tell me to rent something scary?

JOY:

Oh I don't know maybe I was just remembering back to when we used to watch scary movies and I'd get scared and you'd give me a little comfort. Forgive me if I was just trying to get a little contact.

EDDY:

Shut up.

JOY:

Well it's true. (*to audience*) Ever since he quit smoking. I mean if it's going to mean a bit of contact for me I say just smoke.

EDDY:

Oh that's helpful. Thanks a lot for your support. It's not f'ing easy.

JOY:

Oh I know I know I know all about it. Anyways. The interesting thing was—when I heard the sound—without even knowing I knew it was coming from Leonard's.

EDDY:

Leonard was the fag across the street.

JOY:

Eddy!

EDDY:

What?

JOY:

You can't call him that.

EDDY:

Why not? He called himself that.

JOY:

But you can't say it unless you are it. You have to be it to say it. If you're not it and you say it it's degrading. You can't say it unless you are it. Unless you are it. Maybe that's why I'm not getting any contact.

EDDY:

Shut up.

JOY:

Well I'm not.

EDDY:

Like they need that information. What are you going to tell them next, how big my dick is?

JOY:

(*indicates small*) Eddy I wouldn't.

EDDY:

What?

JOY:

Nothing nothing. Anyways, the thing is, Leonard was a really good neighbour. Not a bit of bother at all.

EDDY:

Oh come on, he was a trouble-maker.

JOY:

He was not.

EDDY:

He was so. He made me cancel the street hockey tournament. I had fifteen fellas from work signed up.

JOY;

Oh for God's sake Eddy, street hockey tournament, it was just an excuse for a big booze up. (*to audience*) He put his back out anyway.

EDDY:

He wouldn't let us barbecue!

JOY:

Well not in the front yard Eddy! Who barbecues in the front yard? What kind of neighbourhood would it be if everybody was out barbecuing in the front yard! You don't barbecue in the front yard. That's what back yards are for. (*to the audience*) He's a savage.

EDDY:

Whatever.

JOY:

(*to EDDY*) He wasn't such a trouble-maker when he was paying for the cocktails though was he? (*to audience*) Leonard used to have us over some weekends in the summer for cocktails. You never brought a bottle.

EDDY:

Whatever.

JOY:

Whatever whatever. And what a beautiful place. The stuff he had. Oh my God. And the books, my dear you wouldn't believe the books. A dozen shelves just books, not a knick-knack on 'em. And all these beautiful beautiful masks from Mexico with all this beautiful beautiful beadwork—and hand-painted—beautiful. Oh God I'd love to get to Mexico. (*a look to EDDY*) Yes well. Oh what a place, put together in the most exquisite way like out of a magazine. Leonard was a very sensitive soul.

EDDY:

You think so?

JOY:

What?

EDDY:

Well not if you believe what you read in the paper.

JOY:

Oh for God's sake Eddy.

EDDY:

Well that's what it said in the paper. (*to audience*) The go on over there I guess it was scandalous. The sex and the drugs. All sorts of unsavoury types in and out of there day and night. Computer full of porn.

JOY:

Oh Eddy shut up.

EDDY:

That's what it said in the paper.

JOY:

All you need to say something in the paper is a big mouth and some ink.

EDDY:

You don't want to be talking to us anyway. We hardly knew him. Talk to the ones next door.

JOY:

Virginia and Samuel.

EDDY:

"Samuel."

JOY:

What?

EDDY:

"Samuel" why do we have to call him Samuel, what's wrong with Sam.

JOY:

His name is Samuel, if he wants to be called Samuel call him Samuel, it's his name.

EDDY:

And "Virginia" she's just as bad. One time I called her Ginny you would have thought I stuck my hand up her skirt.

JOY:

Eddy! Savage. They're nice. A little fancy for us but nice. They always have the Christmas party every year for the neighbourhood.

EDDY:

Who cares.

JOY:

Eddy, shut up . But anyways the long and the short of it is that Leonard was a very good person. Period. I don't know why everybody's getting all caught up in this sex business. There's nothing wrong with sex. I like sex. My mother liked sex.

EDDY:

Oh my God like I got to listen to this.

JOY:

Maybe what you really need Eddy is to talk about it.

EDDY:

What?

JOY:

> They got commercials on TV now for it and everything.

EDDY:

> (*to audience*) Listen to what I gotta put up with. That's the go on. You wouldn't believe last year at Thanksgiving, her and her mother sitting at the dinner table talking about sex like it was the weather, like it was Current Affairs.

JOY:

> Well it is Current Affairs for some people Eddy, not like you Ancient History.

EDDY:

> Shut up I'm hungry.

JOY:

> So what?

EDDY:

> I'm just saying I'm hungry.

JOY:

> Then make yourself a sandwich.

EDDY:

> All right I will.

JOY:

> All right then do.

EDDY:

> All right then fine.

JOY:

> All right then fine.

EDDY:

> All right goodbye.

JOY:

All right goodbye.

EDDY:

(*to audience*) Good luck.

JOY:

Shut up. Good God. He's exhausting.
Anyways. I like sex. My mother liked sex.
There's nothing wrong with sex. And I don't
just mean religiously and all that with one
person for your whole life. No. I played
around a bit before I met Eddy. Why not.
And I'm not going to say I didn't have a
tingle or two when we moved in here and I
saw Samuel next door. God forgive me. Not
that I would though—Eddy's enough for
me—if he'd ever get around to being enough
again—I settle for less than "enough"—I'd
settle for "a little"—I'd settle for "some." And
don't take Eddy the wrong way. He comes off
like a bit of an arsehole but that's just when
there's people around. He's fine when he's
alone. And him and Leonard got along good.
Oh yeah one time Eddy went over and fixed
Leonard's washer, they were there all
afternoon talking, drinking coffee, smoking
cigarettes.

I don't believe what they put in the papers.
Let them have their gossip and their taudry
talk I won't have any part of it. Live and let
live. People get mixed up. It happens. And
the world today. You look at the young
people. It's all sex and drugs and drugs and

sex ... I mean it was in my day too. And when our daughter Trisha was in high school I'd find the odd thing lying around. I'd have a little puff. Don't tell Eddy for God's sake he'd have me in a rehab. But now it's all crazy. Especially the sex. The kids today. Going home from school, instead of going home they're sneaking off to somebody or other's basement where the parents are split up or working and they're down there popping pills and having group sex when they should be smoking cigarettes and heavy petting. There's nobody to say what's what. There's no good examples. And in the case of what happened to Leonard ... Well it must be hard for two men, with a man and a woman there's the woman there to sort of balance things out, for two men it must be so hard ... (*laughs*) Well that's it, it's always hard for the men— but for Eddy. (*laughs*) Oh I shouldn't laugh. It must be difficult. But with Leonard I don't think it had anything to do with sex at all. I think he was just lonely. People get lonely God knows. Anyways.

EDDY:

Are you still talking about sex.

JOY:

I thought you were making yourself a sandwich.

EDDY:

I did.

JOY:

And you ate it?

EDDY:

Yeah.

JOY:

That fast.

EDDY:

What?

JOY:

No wonder you're always complaining you got indigestion. And you never made me one?

EDDY:

You didn't say you wanted one.

JOY:

Fine fine.

EDDY:

You want me to make you a sandwich? (*burps*) I'll make you a sandwich.

JOY:

No fine fine. I shouldn't eat this late anyways.

EDDY:

Anyways.

JOY:

Anyways.

EDDY:

I remember the sound. And that it was Sunday night.

JOY:

It was Monday morning.

EDDY:

It's not morning if you haven't gone to bed yet.

JOY:

No.

EDDY:

And you were still up watching the end of that foolish movie.

JOY:

Maybe. I guess it was closer to two.

EDDY:

2:02.

JOY:

I remember the sound.

Light shift.

LEONARD:

Island people. How's that for sophisticated. Make me look pretty oh la la. And she did love to talk about sex. It was her favourite topic of discussion. Followed closely by her dream of going to (*pronounced phonetically:*) "Porta Va*ll*arta." I didn't bother to correct her though. So I just called it Porta Vallarta too. Which when I think of it was probably the highlight of my generosity as a neighbour. Oh I shouldn't be so hard on myself. Hey maybe that's Eddy's problem he's hard on himself. And he never fixed my washer thank you very much. Oh he came over and he smoked all my cigarettes and drank all my coffee and regaled me with tales of his high school exploits—he left and the washer still didn't work. Five hundred dollars later it was a loose wire—ah but what does he know about loose wires he's a plumber. He was right about the time though, 2:02 and fifty-eight, fifty-nine, 2:03.

Thunder—light shift.

And the sound continues through the bedroom, down the stairs, into the den, mixing in with sound of the scary movie, and out under the back door into the rain which is helped along now by an easterly wind. You'd think that such a sound, such a low strange sound such as this, might get lost in the rain—splintered in the drops. But this is not the case. It rides the wind through the rain, sweeping around the still bright house of Samuel and Virginia and on to the dark house at the end of the street and in through the open window. Open even in the rain. The sound pooling there on the sill of the open window. Pooling with the rain. On the sill of the open window.

BICK:

2:03. I was up. Not up but awake. It made me think of the cat. The sound. I heard it because I had the window open. I still do. Sleep. With the window open. It wasn't me though. I never did like it. Sleeping. With the window open. That was her. Doreen. She used to. Like to. Sleep. With the window open. I never did. I'd have to get up so early.

37

So I'd be in bed first. Close the window. Go
to bed. Fall asleep. She'd come up. Doreen.
Open up the window. Go to bed. Fall asleep.
I'd wake up. Freezing. Get up. Close the
window. Go to bed. Fall asleep. She'd wake
up. Get up. Open the window. Back to bed.
Fast asleep. I'd wake up. Freezing. Close the
window. Open the window close the window
open the window. Back and forth back and
forth just like that the whole night through.
Went on like that. I don't know. Years.
Eventually though I just gave up. It was my
feet mainly. Would get cold. So I just took to
sleeping in socks. Let her have her open
window. I did get back at her though. From
time to time. I'd leave the seat up on
purpose. Never did admit it was on purpose.
She suspected but never did admit she did. I
think she enjoyed it. The tit for tat. Bit of a
scrapper she was. Doreen. Good bit of a sense
of humour too. Gone now what? I don't
know. Years. Funny thing is. Don't have to
anymore but still do. Sleep with the window
open. Funny. She'd enjoy that.

But you're not here about Doreen are you.
You're here about the cat. And I'm sorry …
Oh no you're not here about the cat, shut up,
you're here about the Leonard fellow. Yes.
Well I didn't know him. He used to catch my
eye once from time to time. I'd be out
working the lawn. He'd always give me the
Doctor. "Doctor Bickford." I never did bother
to correct him. Bickerson.

Bick. Bickerson. Bick Bickerson. Bick. Just
Bick. Or Bicker. Or Bickerson. Or Ernie.
Bickerson. But Bick. Just Bick. Bick stuck.
Used to play a bit of hockey and Bickerson
wouldn't fit on the back of the jersey so it was
just Bick and Bick stuck. I wanted "Doc." Hey
Doc. How ya doin' Doc. Nice shot Doc. But
oh no, no one was having any of that. Not for
the lowly old veterinarian. No veterinarians
don't get the doctor too easy. No room for
that kind of respect for the poor old lowly old
veterinarian. Chiropractors have that
complaint too I hear. And dentists. But not
proctologists. No, you're pretty quick to give
your proctologist the Doctor, but I guess
you'd be in a position to give that kind of
respect being the position you'd have to be in
to be in that position. You know. Not to say I
cared I suppose. I did enjoy my work.
Thoroughly. No indeed I did. Never did want
to retire. But they do that to you don't they.
And retire to what? To being the crusty old
fart at the end of the street who's always after
the kids to get off the lawn. I never gave a
hoot and a half about my lawn until I retired.
Now I know more about sod than I ever knew
about dogs. Honestly. But one thing is,
interesting, you've got to be careful of the
seams. In the sod. Even when the sod takes
root you've got to be careful of the seams.
The water will still tend to gather at the seam
and if you don't watch out you'll get a bit of
rot. That's those brown patches you see. Ken

Turner's got a bit of that on his, though that could also be due to—that hedge they put in—Shut up.

No never cared too much for dogs. It was cats was more my thing. And that's what I thought it was. That sound. That strange low sound that night. It was the sound of like when you put a cat down. And that's a sound I know pretty damn well I must say because I did put a fair number down in my time. And that would be the sound—of course sometimes there'd be nothing at all. Just a bit of a jerk or a spasm. But other times there'd be the sound. Oh they'd bring in the poor old thing all crippled up and suffering "Can you do something for my poor little guy?" Yes I can, I can do something for him I can put him out of his misery. The cat would be looking up at me with his eyes all full of "Kill me kill me." But they wouldn't see it. People. They just don't want to let go. They hang on and hang on till there's nothing but skin and bones. It all happened very fast with the cats. But for the sound. And don't take this strange but in some ways it could be a quite beautiful sound. This little noise, like this little ball of air, almost with some weight to it, this little ball of life you could almost just almost just hold. Like that, this little ball of sound, this little ball of life like that in your hand. Just like that and pass it back and forth just like that … just like that … But now it's all … Gone. Where? Gone the way of the letter from London that's where it's gone. I was in London. Years years years ago. Just after Doreen and I were married. I was in London, Doreen was here. I had a nice place, little room up on the second floor looking down into the park. And every Sunday I'd sit at my desk in the window and write my letter home looking down into the park, and the same father and son always there in their suits from church, a ball between them, those bushes with the … what are they called, those red and yellow blossoms, lovely little birdsong … Sitting there in the window, at your desk, your clean piece of paper and your good pen, writing your letter home, line by line, word by word, thought by thought. Or maybe just one thought. So much just what happened, this happened Tuesday, and a nice restaurant on Wednesday, and who said what to who on Thursday, and just so much what happened and then maybe just one good, one real thought. Maybe just at the end of the letter. Maybe just "I miss you." "I miss you." And then you sign it, and you fold the paper and you fold it twice, and you put it in the stiff new envelope and you lick it—with your very own wet, your very own from your mouth from your own personal personal person. And you seal it and you turn it over and oh you don't have a stamp. Okay. Put on your jacket, go downstairs, walk to the corner then right at the butcher's, a special trip to the post office, go in, up to the counter, give your money to the fellow—heavy that money—and he gives you the stamp and you lick it—with the stuff of yourself, DNA all over that. And you put the stamp on the front of the envelope. The stiff new envelope with the address there and you give it to the man in his hand and he puts it in a box. And then another fellow takes it from the box in his hand and gives it to another fellow in his hand to another fellow in his hand and to a hand to a hand to a hand. This lovely little thought, this little ball of life, just like that. And now it's just, like this. And the time. The time. That's the difference of it the time. Two weeks it takes to get there. Two real, long, solid weeks later and it gets there and she opens it and two weeks later and it's all still there. The Tuesday this happened and the Wednesday night restaurant and Thursday who said what to who and the father and the son in their Sunday suits and the blossoms and the birdsong and two weeks later and I still miss you. I miss you. I miss you more than ever. Two weeks later and it's still true. Truer.

But now it's just ticka ticka ticka (a *farting sound as he presses "send" on an imaginary keyboard*). It takes time to be true. No, no more letters from London anymore. No more little balls of life ... And I guess that's what I was thinking about when I heard it. The sound, that night. That. And the cat. Or the cat come back. Or I don't know. I'm sorry. It wasn't my place to … just that Leonard fellow seemed like the type that would just hang on and hang on … And I'm sorry about the Leonard fellow too. He used to catch my eye from time to time. I'd be out working on the lawn. He'd always give me the Doctor. I appreciated that.

I've had a thought, sure I have. Shut up. Oh we all think we're all so different. Then you get to a point when you realize that no matter who you are there's really only the same five things that happen to everybody.

Pause.

I guess you're going to want me to tell you what they are now.

Birth, death, love, weather and arthritis. But by the time you realize that, your hips are too seized up to enjoy it, and it's probably raining anyway.

Yes I've had a thought … In my hockey days, sure, road trip, out of town game, there'd be that once in a while, bit of a skirmish on the ice, you'd be up against the boards with a fellow—close like that in the corner, shoulder to shoulder, catch his eye he'd catch yours. Later at the bar, having a drink, catch his eye again. Sure, I've had a thought. It's not the end of the world.

I hear the people who bought the empty house have kids. That'll be nice. Haven't been kids around here in a while. I'm a little out of practice. (*yelling gruffly*) "Hey you kids get off the damn lawn."

Ah to hell with it, who cares about the goddamn lawn anymore. I'm just the old fucker at the end of the street who sleeps with his socks on and the window open.

Light shift.

LEONARD:

Isn't he a sweetie. Yeah. He killed my cat. I don't want to talk about it. I'm sure someone will tell you the story. Oh well. There but for the grace of whoever. Poor old cat killer. And Doreen? Tough cookie. Sense of humour? Oh yeah. Like a nail gun. Nail gun? What do I know about nail guns? (*looks at his fingernails*) Oh well, nail gun! Patent that. I hear they keep growing. Talk to me in a month. What time does that make it?

Thunder—light shift.

2:04. And now the sound might just be the wind. Something you hear but think you don't hear at all. Like the secret sound in a lover's voice that tells you your lover doesn't love you anymore. The kind of sound you won't hear for fear of what it might be. Just the wind. And it might have been if it weren't for the music. A tiny line of music that rises up just lightly underneath the sound, lifting it from its pool gathering on the windowsill. Lifting it up, gently gently and nudging it lightly into the night. Gently gently. Almost floating now. The sound held just above the little line of music, carried gently gently in a kind of a curving motion between and around the now intermittent drops of rain. The sound now the music, the music now the sound. Pausing only briefly to land, gently gently in the ear of Virginia.

Light shift.

VIRGINIA:

(*sings*) "Oh here is love and here is truth."

Poor Leonard. At least he had something beautiful to listen to in his final moments.

The Pirates of Penzance. G and S. Gilbert and Sullivan. Oh what a delightful, what a rollicking, what a roll in the good times they are. Oh the music, the patter, the story lines, stop it! God bless G and S. I certainly wouldn't call myself an aficionado though. Samuel certainly could—he wouldn't though he's too too far too self-effacing for that—but he most certainly is. Samuel and I met doing a Gilbert and Sullivan. Years ago with the ADL? The Amateur Drama League? It was a lesser known work called *Patience,* or *Bunthorne's Bride.* Due to a lack of gentlemen in the league I was cast as Reginald Bunthorne, listed in the dramatis personae as "a fleshy poet." Samuel was our musical direc-tor and pianist. Shortly after our meeting Samuel discovered not only a prediliction for the piano but also a rather sublime aptitude for bringing rapture to the larger lady. Oh our romance may have begun as furtive frottage behind the flats but it soon found itself centre stage drowning in a rain of roses and bravas. Yes but let's leave all that to the fullness of time and my memoirs shall we? Suffice it to say we landed here cozy and content on our charming if eclectic dead end street.

But perhaps in deference to Leonard's memory I should refer to it as a cul-de-sac.

We didn't know Leonard very well. It was Robert more we clicked with, Leonard's ex-boyfriend. Robert was a whirling dervish of wit and mischievousness while Leonard was more … less complicated. Let's just say where Robert was the *New York Times* crossword Leonard was more a search-a-word-puzzle—it was all sort of given, you just had to circle the letters. Robert did the most outlandish windows for The Bay downtown—my word—and when December rolled around, ladies hold on to your hats. The three wise men in rainbow afros and the baby Jesus with big false eyelashes Miraculously inventive. But you go by The Bay on the holidays and what is it? "Have a very DKNY Christmas." About as inventive as a glass of tap water. Of course to be fair to Leonard, anyone would have paled in Robert's glare. He used to do—Robert used to do these brilliant drag-show-cum-performance-art-events at this horrible little local they insisted on frequenting—The Gear Box or something equally greasy. Robert's

Carmen Miranda was a revelation in hilarity. And at the end you could eat the fruit! Little did I know when I introduced Robert to an acquaintance of mine, a very charming, very sophisticated antiques dealer from South Beach, that sparks would fly—and fly they did. And I must admit that I did encourage Robert in his decision to leave Leonard. But Robert seemed destined for so much more, he was so cultured and well traveled—I mean Leonard hadn't really ever been anywhere— outside a couple of excursions to, as Leonard called it (*as before, phonetically:*) "Porta Vallarta." He grew up not far from here Leonard did, an unfortunate upbringing I learned from Robert—from foster home to foster home, that sort of thing. It couldn't have been very pleasant. But Leonard seemed to blossom when Robert left. He struck up an adorable friendship with little Madison Turner, Ken Turner's daughter across the street. Madison, she's a precocious little girl. Well she's not so little anymore. Madison used to babysit for Samuel and I when we'd go away weekends—for our little chihuahua—Pipi—before Pipi disappeared. But yes, Madison and Leonard, they were just like that; thick as thieves there for a while.

It's interesting to consider when things began to unravel for Leonard. Oh there was that ridiculous business with the hedge and miserable Ken Turner—Madison's father. Oh Leonard fell upon a book on feng shui. And that was Leonard all over, falling upon some book, oh this was going to change his life, he'd read the introduction and up on the shelf it would go. But feng shui was going to be his new thing and so he bought some round tables and moved this and that around and decided what he really needed was a hedge beside the house to catch all the chi escaping from the kitchen. So lickety split up went the hedge, which turned out to be an encroachment on Ken Turner's property, and Turner went rabid about not having clear access to his back yard, apparently there were court dates set and the whole nine yards ... oh it was just a nothing that turned into a circus.

Of course there was the Christmas party, things did head south after that. We always hold the Christmas party for the neighbourhood. Samuel always looks so forward to hosting it, "Can I get you another egg nog," he's such a Santa. We weren't going to bother last year but decided we should make the effort if only for the sake of the Saeeds since they'd taken to being a bit invisible of late considering the political climate and the fact that they are Muslim. So we thought the least we could do was to extend the friendly hand of neighbourliness. He's a pleasant enough fellow, an eye surgeon, and she's ... well to say she's silent and subservient would be to paint a far more animated portrait than is the actuality. Be that as it may, ahead went the Christmas party which turned out to be an unqualified fiasco due to a kerfuffel which erupted between Leonard and Madison. Oh and it was really just another nothing which Ken Turner blew all out of proportion. You know what else he did, that miserable Ken Turner? Leonard wasn't dead one week and Ken Turner was out there digging up that hedge. Honestly. Lawyers.

And then there was the tragedy of Whiskers. Leonard's cat. Went missing last month, the week before the terrible business with Leonard. Oh Leonard was inconsolable. He'd had Whiskers for eons. But it did bring the neighbourhood together in a way, everyone running about putting tins of cat food hither and thither hoping to lure the poor creature home. Little did we know. I mean that really didn't figure in I suppose since the truth of all that only came out recently. Poor Mr. Bickerson. Apparently nostalgic for his former profession he coerced the unfortunate beast into his basement and put him to sleep. What happens to people? There but for the grace of whomever. Though it does raise a disquieting question or two about the fate of dear Pipi—not to mention Doreen. Yes but the past is just that isn't it.

I do have one lovely memory of Leonard. It was shortly after Leonard and Robert had split and Leonard decided he was going to try his hand at singing. So, he signed up for one of these little variety shows that they would hold at the Grease Factory or whatever it was. And this was so unlike Leonard, Leonard was always one to shun the spotlight—unless he was two glasses of wine beyond his limit and then you mightn't be surprised to find him on the coffee table with his knickers on his noggin—and unfortunately that's no hyperbole. Be that as it may. So Leonard asked Samuel to accompany him in his song and he came over one afternoon to practice and I sat in. Oh it was adorable watching Leonard struggle through the song. An odd little song, something about "If you see my love please don't forget to tell him that I'm sorry that he ever met you." Rather oblique, opaque, obtuse, obscure.

But a perfectly passable voice. Not a big voice but a sweet voice, a simple voice … an honest voice.

Of course he could have used more support here, and he was somewhat tone deaf. But that's fixable. I offered him some lessons but he never took me up on it. Never ended up singing the song either, but that was Leonard all over, another book on the shelf never read.

The night it happened I was upstairs in my office working on my memoirs. I seldom sleep before three. Samuel was downstairs putting out a tin of cat food thinking that perhaps poor Whiskers might turn up on our back step as he often had in the past. And then I caught a little bit of "Pirates"— (*singing*) "Oh here is love and here is truth"—and I immediately thought of Leonard. We had given Robert and Leonard a copy of *The Pirates of Penzance* as a Christmas gift some years before. Robert was a huge G and S fan and Leonard seemed drawn to the work as well. All the talk of orphans perhaps. Perhaps. (*singing*) "Oh here is love and here is truth … " And then the music was gone but a sound remained. An odd … a clear … Not a familiar but a very very human sound. Almost a "noooooooo … "

> *Light shift.*

LEONARD:

Robert. He was Robert to Virginia. Robert had a big mouth. I hated Robert.

I was indifferent to Bob. He was Bob to his family.

He was Bobby in bed. He was Bobby to me.

I thought Bobby was going to be my story. Clearly not.

Boo hoo. Who cares.

> *LEONARD turns his back on the audience for several moments. Suddenly turning back:*

Oh here's a piece of information you might be interested in about Virginia and Samuel: nudists.

2:05.

Thunder—light shift.

The sound continues clearer now, stronger now, now an unwavering line, like a string, like a rope, like a hydro wire, across the street and into the tree, through the wet branches, down the trunk. Was that pain? Was that pleasure? Into the ground. Is this real? Am I dreaming? Through the new roots of the hedge. Whiskers? Through the window of her basement bedroom and along the concrete wall, past the desk where the lamp is off but still warm her studying for tomorrow's math test—

Light shift.

MADISON:

(*throughout MADISON plays with a disposable lighter*) Math? Hello? What am I eight? They stop teaching math in grade three. Algebra. And I never said "'The Balsawood Astronaut' was a 'novel'"—I said it was a story. And I wasn't writing it in my journal, I was illustrating it. Adults are such knobs.

"The Balsawood Astronaut" by Madison Paige Turner. I know, what were they thinking? It was just kid stuff.

"The Balsawood Astronaut" by Madison Paige Turner. There once was a balsawood boy who had a very bad life and so he decides to go on a journey and blah blah blah blah blah and on his journey he meets a giant baby who also had a very bad life because he was a giant baby and what can a giant baby do. The giant baby had tried to be a dentist because he thought maybe if the dentist was a giant baby then people wouldn't be so scared to go to the dentist—but would you want a giant baby with a drill in your mouth? So the balsawood boy and the giant baby got together and went on a journey and blah blah blah blah blah and then they met up with the three-faced man who was a judge because he could see things from every angle—except for from behind which is how he got killed when he got run over by the two-door house.

Two-door house. I got that from Meryl—my mom—she was saying how she wanted to live in a Tudor house and thought she was saying a "two-door house" and I said "Don't all houses have two doors." Apparently that was "cute." Tudor house. Adults are such knobs.

Of course, it is, inevitable, that I too, shall one day, become, a knob. But not yet. No I still have my whole life ahead of me. And what's that, let's see: burning babies, falling buildings, the war on war and you can't wash your hair in tap water or it will turn to dust and fall out. Thanks a lot knobs. And then what? You get old and move to Florida. Or turn into big-dick-Bick-Bickerson-Cat-Killer. I think he did the right thing though. Leonard never would have done it. Whiskers was

ancient. Whiskers was dust. I think Whiskers
wanted to die.

Old men have huge scrotums.

That's so dirty what you're thinking. I'm
just a little girl. Leonard told me. Leonard
wasn't a knob most of the time. But he wasn't
really like an adult though. Not like he was
like a kid but more like he was, I don't know
—corny—an equal—corny—. I mean he
would actually ask my opinion about things—
and not in that condescending kind of
pointless kind of liberal parenting kind of
way like: "Would you like to live with Mommy
or Daddy after the divorce Brittany, Jessica,
Christina, Alliyah, Madison, Paige, Turner."
What were they thinking? That's what
happens when you're born into a family of
lawyers. Both of them. Meryl doesn't practice
anymore, now she does pilates full time. She
was never really a lawyer lawyer though—she
was one of those saint lawyers who only
represented single mother drug addict
strippers and their pimps. Ken is more of the
regular type son of a bitch lawyer. He's always
saying how lawyers get a bad rap. He tries to
compare lawyers to surgeons. He says, "Well if
I was a surgeon and a killer came in with a
knife in his head I shouldn't take the knife
out of his head because he's a killer?" Hello?
The analogy doesn't work Ken! Because if
surgeons were like lawyers they'd just turn to
the guy with the knife in his head and say

"You don't have a knife in your head buddy" and charge him two thousand dollars. Son of a bitch. I got that off Meryl. That's what she calls Ken. "That son of a bitch." "You son of a bitch." "He's a son of a bitch." I asked her but she said it was in no way a reference to my grandma. My grandma's cool. She's old. She lives in Florida. Florida's full of old people and Disneyworld. Discuss.

The son of a bitch stole my journal! I'm sure it was him. And only probably because he was sure it was full of sex. They're obsessed with sex. Meryl's always trying to talk to me about sex. It's so embarrassing. Please. I know all about sex. But I haven't had sex. Mouth doesn't count. The former president of the United States said so. Liberals are such knobs.

Leonard hardly ever talked about sex. I mean he did but not in the educational way. They said his computer was full of porn but it so wasn't and if it was it was his boyfriend's. His boyfriend was such a knob. He was so gay. And I mean that in the bad way. Plus he was very "flamboyant." Flamboyant that's so 2002 …

The son of a bitch can take away my cigarettes but he's not getting my lighter.

I taught Leonard how to smoke. We used to smoke in his kitchen. I mean he smoked but he just didn't hold it right. He held it like it was dirty. You've got to love it. Kiss it. You've got to say yes to the cigarette. I taught Leonard how to smoke and he taught me ... He helped me with my public speaking contest subject. HIV is not the cause of AIDS.

"HIV is not the cause of AIDS. There is no proof that HIV causes AIDS. All the epidemiological and microbiological evidence taken together conclusively demonstrates that HIV does not cause AIDS or any other illness. The concept that AIDS is caused by a virus is not a fact, but a theory that was introduced at a 1984 press conference by Dr. Robert Gallo, a researcher employed by the National Institutes of Health i.e.: the American government ... " Blah blah blah blah blah.

Leonard was into all that HIV stuff. He had HIV. But he didn't tell most people because most people are such knobs. I was helping him surf the day he found that website, HIV is not the cause of AIDS. He was so excited, he kept saying "I'm not going to die of AIDS." And he didn't. But he still died though.

HIV is not the cause of AIDS ...

I plagiarized that right off the web site. And why not. Leonard even said. It wasn't a public writing contest it was a public speaking contest. It wasn't about how I wrote it it was about how I spoke it. And I came third. Out of sixteen. But that wasn't good enough for Ken. He's relentless "You should have written it yourself you might have won." I did win, I came third out of sixteen, that's still winning—coming 16th out of 16 that's not winning coming third out of sixteen that's winning. "But you could have come first with a little more effort." Ken's relentless.

It was like when I made this two-minute video for social sciences and I showed it to Ken and he got all Roger Ebert on me. It was a video of Whiskers chewing a Barbie. I wasn't trying to make *The Matrix*. He's relentless. "Maybe if you'd picked another subject." Oh yeah, he wanted me to do "Why Is Law Important" (*yawn*) yeah right "Why Are Adults Knobs." He wanted me to do "What is Autism." Oh my God. I used to be autistic. It wasn't really autism though, they didn't find out until later what it was. It was Asperger's. Asperger's Asperger's. Assburger's. Assburger's. I'll have two ass burgers please. Wax those buns ... Asperger's is a syndrome which is mainly characterized by the child not seeming to grasp the concept that conversation is reciprocal. That was fun while it lasted. I got over the Asperger's though, I snapped out of it when Ken and Meryl split up. Out of relief. Why bother. All the epidemiological and microbiological evidence taken together conclusively demonstrates that marriage does not work. Does not. Does not work. Does not work. Ric-o-la. Does not work! Everybody's always happier when they're split up or divorced or on their own. Even Leonard—when his boyfriend left—at first he was sad but after a while he was happier. He even said so.

I wish I could be a lesbian. It would be easier. Girls are easier. I mean girls can be bitchy but so can boys just when boys are bitchy they call it highly motivated. A lesbian. Maybe that's what I'll be when I grow up. Maybe I could do it on career day. "Hey where do I sign up to spend the day with a lesbian?" They'd probably let me too, the liberals.

Coming third is good. Leonard thought so. To celebrate took me out to dinner at Swiss Chalet. As he often did. We had an excellent conversation. As we often did. He said to me "You can be my story now." I didn't know what it meant, but it was nice.

Sometimes people just want to die. It's easier if you think that.

Want to see something?

LEONARD:

She lifts up her t-shirt sleeve and shows a tattoo.

MADISON:

It's p'ing, the Chinese symbol for peace. It's the end of the world. Thanks a lot knobs.

I haven't had solid food in three days. Unless cock counts. That's so dirty. I'm just a little girl. How could I anyway? I'm grounded. For saying "freak." For saying "freak"! Because I'm not allowed to say (fuck) so I

58

don't say (fuck) I don't say (fuck) and even though I have many opportunities to say (fuck) I don't say (fuck) and instead of saying (fuck) I say "freak." Like: "Freak off" or "I freaked up" or "Hey are those two dogs freaking?" And Ken's all still coming down on me and I'm like "I'm just saying 'freak'!" and he's all: "It's not the word it's the intention."

Intention. Intention. Detention. Attention. Attention. Attention.

She lights the lighter. She tries to grab the flame.

Sometimes I'm not even sure if I miss Leonard. Sometimes I'm not even sure if I have any feelings at all. —Corny—. I'm such a knob.

And then one day the balsawood boy is all by himself. And he thinks and he thinks and he thinks what he could do to make his life better. What in the world could be the purpose of his life? What in the world is he good at? Better than anyone? What is it that makes him special. And then he realizes. He's made of balsawood. He can float. And that's when the balsawood boy knows that one day he will become the balsawood astronaut.

The title kind of gives the ending away.

I'm sorry about the Christmas party. That was my fault. I feel bad about that. Well, that's something I feel.

SAMUEL:

Merry Christmas Madison.

MADISON:

Merry Christmas Samuel.

SAMUEL:

Can I get you an eggnog?

MADISON:

No thanks, is Leonard here?

SAMUEL:

I think Leonard is in the kitchen.

MADISON:

Okay see ya.

SAMUEL:

Merry Christmas Ken.

KEN:

(*on phone*) Hey Samuel. I've gotta take this sorry. New receptionist.

SAMUEL:

Not a problem not a problem.

KEN:

(*into phone*) What is his position? What's his position?

SAMUEL:

And how are you doing Bick? Can I get you some more eggnog?

BICK:

I wouldn't mind if it had a bit of a kick in it.

SAMUEL:

You want a bit of a kick do you Bick? You want a kick Bick?

BICK:

> I'll give you a kick.

SAMUEL:

> Merry Christmas welcome welcome. Merry Christmas Joy.

JOY:

> Merry Christmas Samuel.

SAMUEL:

> Merry Christmas Edward.

EDDY:

> Merry Christmas Sam.

JOY:

> Eddy.

EDDY:

> Samuel.

SAMUEL:

> Not a problem not a problem. Can I get you an eggnog Joy?

JOY:

> Oh I'll get something myself. We picked youse up a CD at the mall. It's Christmas music, like classical like you like but a bit more upbeat.

SAMUEL:

> Well get that to Virginia and she'll put it on.

JOY:

> Okay. I'll be right back. (*to EDDY*) Behave yourself.

EDDY:

> The Mohammeds aren't here?

SAMUEL:

> The Saeeds.

EDDY:

> I thought they were the big guests of honour or whatever.

SAMUEL:

> No they had to go out of town for the weekend.

EDDY:

> Figures they wouldn't show their face around on a Christian holiday.

SAMUEL:

> Can I get you an eggnog Edward.

EDDY:

> You got any beer?

SAMEUL:

> Yes.

EDDY:

> You got Heineken?

SAMUEL:

> We got a keg actually.

EDDY:

> (*leaving*) Right on.

JOY:

> (*returning*) I couldn't find her.

SAMUEL:

> You're not having eggnog Joy?

JOY:

Oh I'm just going to start with a glass of wine, don't want eggnog on an empty stomach. Bloats me.

SAMEUL:

Of course.

JOY:

It's quite the spread she's got there—all those fancy cheeses.

SAMUEL:

Yes she went all out this year.

JOY:

Did she ever. I'm just going to run upstairs to the little girl's room.

SAMUEL:

Oh we're using the powder room downstairs this year Joy—Reno's a week behind. Rotten timing.

JOY:

You're redoing the bathroom? You just did the kitchen last summer.

SAMUEL:

No rest for the wicked.

JOY:

Honestly. Oh there she is. Virginia! Virginia! Oh she lost weight.

SAMUEL:

No …

VIRGINIA:

Merry Christmas Joy.

JOY:

> Merry Christmas Virginia. We got you a little Christmas CD—it's right up your alley but with a little pizzazz.

VIRGINIA:

> Oh well thank you.

SAMUEL:

> You'll just have to put that on Virginia.

VIRGINIA:

> Oh yes I will. (*moving to leave*) Edward.

EDDY:

> (*returning*) Virginia.

JOY:

> (*to EDDY*) They're redoing their bathroom.

EDDY:

> That's nice. Mohammeds aren't here, as you predicted.

JOY:

> Eddy shut up. (*to SAMUEL*) I'll be right back— (*to EDDY*) behave yourself.

> *A moment of silence between EDDY and SAMUEL.*

EDDY:

> Beer's skunky.

SAMUEL:

> Oh. Perhaps it's just the top of the keg.

EDDY:

> Top of the keg? I don't think so. I've heard of the bottom of the keg being skunky but not the top of the keg. Unless the whole damn keg's skunky.

SAMUEL:

> Yes well I'm sure you'll find out.

EDDY:

> Pardon me?

> > *JOY returns out of breath.*

> That was fast.

JOY:

> Yeah. I just had to wash my hands. Samuel I couldn't help but notice all those fancy cheeses she's got there.

SAMUEL:

> Yes Joy you mentioned—

JOY:

> Is that in honour of the Baby Cheeses?

SAMUEL:

> Oh very good Joy …

JOY:

> I just thought of that one in the bathroom. I really did have to pee. But sometimes if I get a good one and I pee I lose it so I had to rush right back. You got to rush back for the good ones.

SAMUEL:

> That was a good one.

JOY:

> Did you hear that one Eddy?

EDDY:

> Joy why do you come off so stupid, you don't come off half this stupid at home.

JOY:

Shut up areshole.

SAMUEL:

Touché Joy.

JOY:

What?

VIRGINIA:

Is everything all right?

JOY:

Yes wonderful. Virginia girl, you lost weight.

VIRGINIA:

No …

JOY:

I couldn't help but notice all those fancy cheeses.

VIRGINIA:

Yes and help yourself to the—

JOY:

Is that in honour of the Baby Cheeses?

VIRGINIA:

Pardon me?

JOY:

The Baby … Cheeses.

VIRGINIA:

Sorry … Baby?

EDDY:

Jesus, cheeses like Jesus.

VIRGINIA:

That's a good one Eddy.

JOY:

It's mine.

VIRGINIA:

Oh Joy, aren't you the punster.

JOY:

Huh. Oh this is it this is it listen listen listen.

JOY's CD plays a Muzak version of "Silent Night."

SAMUEL listens.

VIRGINIA listens.

EDDY listens.

JOY:

Isn't it great!

VIRGINIA:

Such an interesting …

SAMUEL:

Arrangement.

JOY:

I just love it. I think we'll be doing some dancing tonight.

JOY bumps into EDDY.

EDDY:

Watch it Joy.

BICK:

What the hell is this?

JOY:

It's "Silent Night."

BICK:

I know but what the hell is it.

JOY:

(*loudly*) It's a CD Mister Bickerson! A CD!

BICK:

(*grunts and leaves*)

JOY;

(*calling after*) Mister Bickerson, what do you make of all the cheeses Mister Bick— Anyhoo. Leonard's not a no show is he?

SAMUEL:

No he's in the kitchen with Madison. Virginia why don't you get them in.

VIRGINIA:

Okey dokey.

EDDY:

Madison, she's really growing up isn't she.

JOY:

Shut up Eddy.

EDDY:

What I'm just making an observation.

JOY:

Yeah from your dirty mind.

EDDY:

How come I'm the one with the dirty mind, you're the one wants to get into bondage.

SAMUEL:

Yes well, I was speaking with Leonard this morning and he's come up with what I think is an absolutely capital idea.

EDDY:

Oh great we're starting with the charades all ready.

JOY:

>Forget charades, (*to SAMUEL*) this year we're dancing.

SAMUEL:

>Uh.

VIRGINIA:

>Here they are.

SAMUEL:

>Fine then are we all here?

KEN:

>Quid pro bono? What the hell does that mean? Quid pro bono.

MADISON:

>Ken.

KEN:

>Madison. I'm on the phone!

MADISON:

>Everyone's waiting.

KEN:

>(*on phone*) Hang on, Hang on. (*to group*) Go ahead.

SAMUEL:

>Fine then. Now I don't think we need to point out that there are certain divisions which exist in our neighbourhood and Leonard has come up with an idea that I think might just be the ticket to bring us all together. Leonard, would you like to?

LEONARD:

>(*indicates no*)

SAMUEL:

> Fine then. All we'd have to do is get together as a group and make a kind of proposal to the city and ask that they remove the rather foreboding "Dead End" sign which announces the street and have them replace it with the far more pleasant "Cul-de-sac."

> *Light shift.*

MADISON:

> Cul-de-sac means "arse of the bag." You probably knew that. But Leonard didn't. And so I pointed it out, at the Christmas party. In front of everybody. And they all laughed. And Leonard got embarrassed and so I called him a "knob" and he hated that because he knew that was the worst thing to be. So he hit me. Not hard, just like you'd do to a friend, just like a slap, just like that, on the arm, just like you would with your friend. But it's not the kind of thing you do to a kid in a room full of knobs, especially when the kid's father is there. And Ken goes ballistic. "Take your hands off my daughter." "My daughter." He got all dad-like, which he never did. So I played it up a bit. "Owww." It didn't really hurt and Leonard knew it didn't. And sometimes when you lie and someone knows you're lying, and if in the moment of the lie you don't look at the person who knows you're lying it sometimes makes it hard to ever look at them again.

Ken's not a son of a bitch all the time. One thing was: after Leonard died I kept getting upset every time I looked at the hedge so I asked him to get rid of it and my dad went out and dug it up. That was nice.

And the balsawood astronaut has his first mission to space—his mission to Jupiter—and all systems are go and the engines fire and the rocket is launched but he never made it to Jupiter because as soon as he left the earth's atmosphere he burnt up into ash—because he was just made of balsawood ...

When I heard the sound it didn't sound scary to me. I thought it might have been Whiskers ... Or I thought maybe Leonard got lucky.

Light—sound shift.

ERIC:

He did cunt. Spin it Mister Bitch. (*bar/dance music*)

You looking for some entertainment? How about some Eric-tainment! And that's a little bit of this. And a little bit of this. And a whole lot of this. Turn it up Mister Bitch. Yeah. You want it? You want it? Then you're going to have to pay for it because Eric is prime rib, Eric is prime time, Eric is primo fucking real estate. Yes! Eric is the boy who put the Drive Shaft on the map and the party's just starting. Cut it Mister Bitch. (*music shift*)

Welcome to the Drive Shaft—the centre of the Universe—yeah for big fags and fag hags

71

and bar rags. You want me now? You want me now? Sorry I'm busy—you go talk to Mister Bitch—he'll do you for ten bucks and give you change. Unless you want him to take his teeth out. That's fifteen. Mister Bitch is a genius with his teeth out.

(*shows tattoo*) You know what that is? You know what that is? It's chink for fuck you.

See this watch? (*takes watch out of his pocket and puts it on*) See this watch man! This is my watch, this is my fucking watch. I fucking earned this watch. And I name the price and I set the time and when that buzzer goes I'm gone with the cash and if you're not done you can finish yourself off that's your fucking business. I earned this fucking watch man. The sad old fag, the end of the night he's digging and digging and he pulls out twenty-five bucks. Fuck? What? Twenty-five bucks? (*Note: this number should reflect the top ticket price the audience paid for* Cul-de-sac.) What's that? Half a bag of shitty crystal and a box of Smarties. Fuck that shit. Give me your twenty-five bucks and your fucking watch and a take that—

Hit me in the stomach, hit me in the stomach, hit me in the stomach as hard as you can. That's the old man. I'm like this. (*indicates: small*) He's like this. (*indicates: big*) Hit me in the stomach, hit me in the stomach, hit me in the stomach, hit me in the stomach. So I'm wailing on him I'm wailing on him. He doesn't budge and he's laughing and he hauls off and lets me have it—across the room and out the door and I'm gone. I learned my lesson man, I only had to learn once. He wasn't even my real old man he was just banging my old lady. Old lady MacDonald's. Whore. Billions served. Whore. What the fuck are you looking at?

Here's how it works: no touching, no kissing, no pictures, no video, I keep my boots on, you suck it, you pay me a hundred bucks, I'm gone. Works for me. And I'm telling my fucking girlfriend—if that's what the fags want no skin off my bag—hey fuck I bring home three four bills every night— what the fuck does she want: "Hey I hear you're back at the 7-11—Oh yeah it's great. I even get to wear a uniform!" And flipping burgers and driving your fucking car around the block and valet parking it up your fucking ass. Here's your fucking keys man.

No way man they're lining up for me here. But not for long man, this is not my home, I'm just passing through. I've got a future. Adult films. This fat fuck from San Francisco, couple of weeks ago I'm sitting on his face for a couple of hours, after he tells me I've got a future in adult films. You bet your fucking boots I do, but I'm going to need two credits: one for me and one for Mister Perfect. Yeah you fucking love me, yeah you fucking love me, liar. I see you I see you.

I see the sad old fag—I see him all night sitting in the shadows until he gets drunk enough. He comes up he's all: "Hi I'm Leonard." Yeah Hi I'm Fuck You. What do you want. "Come on back, come on back, come on back to the cul-de-sac." "Yeah yeah yeah, in a minute man—it's only one—we got an hour to last call. Buy me a beer man buy me a beer."

"I've got beer I've got beer back at the cul-de-sac. Come on back come on back come on back to the cul-de-sac." All right all right then man all right, then buy a couple of bags.

We go, we go we go back to the cul-de-sac. Fuck that shit, cul this fucking sac man I know a dead end when I see one man my sheet's full of them. Fuck! (*rubbing his sinus*) What do they cut this shit with man! Oh fuck—that's why you're not seeing my sweet side tonight. I got a sweet side. I've got my sad story man, it's not easy for a little guy, it's not easy for an orphan, fuck, excuse my language, but everything's going to be all right, going ot be all right. Goddamn Catholic church man—they've got a whole hell of a lot to answer for—if I ever see that priest again man—bastard. Oh yeah you suckers love that shit. No, no sad stories here. Okay one. This one. Rugby man. Rugby! Would have been a star. Rugby. You should have seen me—but this pussy country's all hockey. Fuck. What's that—blades on your feet padding padding padding stick in your hand padding padding padding helmet. No way. Rugby. A pair of shoes a pair of shorts and bring it on!

Hit me in the stomach as hard as you can, hit me in the stomach as hard as you can.

Leonard lays out two lines I do them both. What does he care all he wants is Mister Perfect. I'm waiting on my beer man. Where's my beer? Fucking schnapps what? Fucking Crown Royale what? Where's the fag? In the kitchen chopping up fruit. I didn't say I wanted a fucking salad man. He brings me this shitty spic piss. I don't want fucking fruit in my beer. Where's the fag now? He's in the kitchen making me eggs. I said I didn't want a salad. This fucker's making me eggs. I don't want eggs. He's handing me a plate of eggs. I don't want fucking eggs.

ERIC moves as if to smash the plate. SOUND: plate hits the wall.

And the plate hits the wall. The plate makes this beautiful little dent in the perfect blue wall. This beautiful little perfect little slice in the wall. Perfect blue. All these fucking books. What's in all these books man? Are there that many words to make all these books. After a while they must all just sound the same. And then he's showing me this other book—with all these weird drawings, of like space men and babies and shit. He he's saying "I took it but it's not stealing right, she was going to burn it, I saved it, it's not stealing, I saved it from the fire, it's not stealing if you save it from the fire." You saved it from the fire yeah. This fag's fucked man. And all these faces all over the walls looking at me, eyeballing me, can you turn those faces around man. Now the fag wants me to dance. I danced all night man. No he wants me to dance with him. He puts on this toodle oodle oodle fag music. And he starts "I love you I love you." Shut up with that shit man. "I love you I love you." Hey look just give me my money. Give me my money, yeah yeah I'll stay just I want to settle up now. And the fucker's digging and he comes up with twenty-five bucks. Twenty fucking five bucks. Keep digging man. But that's fucking it twenty-five fucking bucks. This is my fucking night man. Give me the fucking twenty-five bucks and your watch and ... And he's still coming at me. "I love you I love you." Get fucking off me man. "I love you." No you don't shut up. "I love you I love you." Shut up shut up shut up. And he's still coming at me. What do they cut this shit with man. He's got me backed up into the kitchen. Shut up. I love you I love you I love you. Shut up (*stab*) Shut up (*stab*) Shut up shut up shut up shut up (*stab stab stab stab*) Shut up. (*kick*) Liar. (*kick*) Shut up. (*kick kick kick*) Shut up (*hit "stereo": sound out*). Shut up.

Sh sh sh sh man. Cool down. Cool down man. Sh sh. I gotta go. Cool down man. Okay

man I gotta go. Okay you got five minutes.
I'm setting the timer look. Two-oh-one. You
got five minutes so just let me know what you
want. Five minutes.

LEONARD:

He doesn't know what to do. He paces
around. He sits on the sofa for a moment. He
gets up. He crosses the room and opens the
window to get some air. 2:02.

ERIC:

Okay man I haven't got all night so you just
let me know. What do you want. I've got
places to be. Sh man sh.

LEONARD:

He goes up stairs and takes a pee. He goes
into the bedroom and sits on the bed with his
head in his hands. He comes back downstairs.
2:03.

ERIC:

You want some music or something man. You
want some music on the stereo. I'll put some
music on okay.

LEONARD:

He puts some music on the stereo. He paces
around me lying on the floor. He thinks
about sitting me up but he doesn't want to
get blood on his clothes. 2:04.

ERIC:

Hurry up. Ticker's talking man ticker's
talking. I'll do you then, you want I'll do you.
Just roll over. Shit.

LEONARD:

> He goes back upstairs. He pees again. He takes a small clay mask off the wall in the bathroom and puts it in his pocket. He goes back downstairs and stands over me. 2:05.

ERIC:

> Man, stop that man. Stop making that noise man. Stop it. Stop making that noise. Stop it, shut up. Shut up. (*kick*)

LEONARD:

> I shut up.
>
> *The watch alarm goes off.*

ERIC:

> (*looking at the watch*) 2:06 man. Time's up. Gotta go.

LEONARD:

> And he left. Don't worry he didn't get away. They caught him. Evidence. (*takes off watch and puts it in his pocket*) And I didn't love him. Please. Where did that come from. I mean sometimes a person gets overwhelmed with … memory or … I didn't love him. I mean maybe I said it but just because you say it doesn't mean you mean it. Or for God's sake I was blind drunk. It wasn't about love anyway it was about twenty-five bucks.
>
> But you know what is interesting? I'm lying on the floor dying, and you know how they say your life flashes before your eyes? No, not me. I just kept thinking, "Yes." Yes. I'm lying there on the floor, dying, and saying no and thinking. Yes. "Yes." "Yes, this is right." "This

is right." "This is how my story is supposed to end." "Finally I'm on the right page." All those years trying to tell somebody else's story, telling the story I thought I was supposed to be telling and it didn't matter because this is my ending and this is right. This is how my story is supposed to end.

I mean, maybe my ending would have been different if I'd tried harder to like hockey.

But only in that I still would have ended up murdered by a prostitute, the only difference would have been she would have been wearing heels.

You can call it what you like, you can fancy up the neighbourhood but any way you look at it life is still a dead end street.

Music.

I don't really believe that. I just said it because it kind of wrapped things up. It sounded sort of smart. There I go, still trying to be sophisticated. I just don't want to stop talking, because once I stop talking then it's over and you hardly got to know me. Well I guess you got kind of a picture. And if a picture's worth a thousand words, what's a song worth? Twenty-five bucks?

(*he sings*) If you see my love
Please don't forget to
Tell him that I'm sorry
He ever met you
And we do know why
But do we care how

Now it's done we're all
Somehow happy now.
But I keep going back
Though I know I'm run through
See I stall when I fall into
Such a big and happy sadness this
Is this my wake up kiss.

> *He holds the lighter aloft and lights it. He*
> *tries to grab the flame.*

End.